Benjamin BANNEKER

By Lilly Golden

CELEBRATION PRESS
Pearson Learning Group

Contents

Benjamin Banneker's Childhood 3

Banneker's Clock 5

Banneker the Astronomer 6

Banneker's Almanac 8

Banneker's Great Adventure 10

Recommended Reading 14

Glossary 15

Index 16

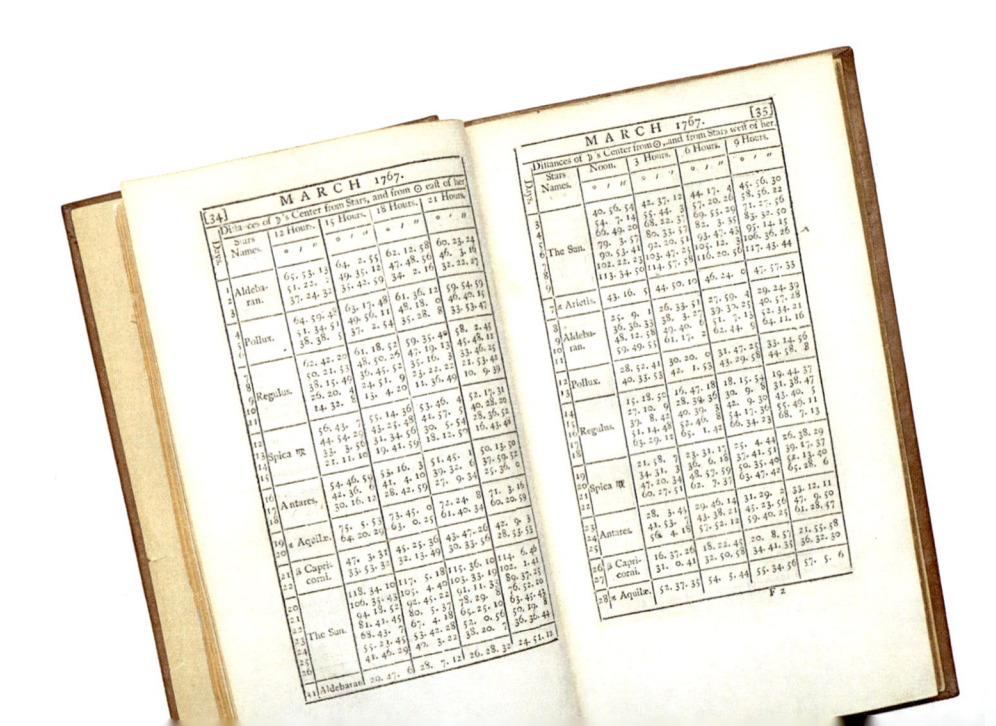

Benjamin Banneker's Childhood

Benjamin Banneker lived more than 200 years ago. He grew up on a farm in Maryland. He never traveled more than 40 miles from his home. Yet, Banneker became a great man. He was the first African American **astronomer** and a mathematician. As an astronomer he studied objects in the sky. As a mathematician, he taught himself the math needed to study the movements of objects in the sky.

Benjamin Banneker (1731–1806), shown on a postage stamp

Banneker's father was a freed slave. Many people at that time did not know how to read or write. However, Banneker's grandmother taught him to read and write when he was very young.

Not only did Banneker know how to read and write, he also understood **math**. At the age of 5 or 6, he helped adults figure out how much money they saved and spent.

Banneker had many interests. He liked to play the flute and the violin. He also loved nature. He watched the Sun, Moon, and stars. He wished he could learn more about them. He wondered why there were sometimes solar **eclipses** and lunar eclipses.

Banneker learned to play the flute and violin at an early age.

Lunar Eclipse

A lunar eclipse happens when Earth is positioned between the Sun and the Moon. Earth blocks the Sun's rays from reaching the Moon. The Moon can look a beautiful red or orange color.

Banneker's Clock

Banneker loved to figure out how things worked. When he was 22 years old, he borrowed a pocket watch. He took it apart and studied each piece. Then he put the watch together again and returned it.

Banneker studied the parts of a pocket watch to build his own clock.

Banneker drew the watch's parts from memory. He multiplied the size of each part to create larger parts. Then, he carved most of the parts from wood to build a clock. When he put it together, the clock worked! It kept perfect time for about 50 years.

Few people in the 1700s had watches or clocks. Many people estimated the time by using sundials.

Banneker the Astronomer

When Banneker was 57 years old, he began to study astronomy. He had help from a neighbor. Banneker and his neighbor, George Ellicott, were good friends. They both loved math and astronomy.

Banneker, a farmer, had no money to buy books. Ellicott had lots of books on astronomy. He loaned Banneker books. Ellicott also loaned Banneker a telescope to study objects in the sky and a compass to show the directions of north, south, east, and west.

Banneker used a telescope similar to this one to study astronomy.

Banneker was very interested in the instruments. The telescope helped him take a closer look at the Moon, planets, and stars.

Banneker was so interested in astronomy that he decided to try to figure out when the next eclipse of the Sun would be. As Banneker worked on his farm, his mind worked on the math problems needed to **predict** the eclipse.

Solar Eclipse

A solar eclipse happens when the Moon passes between Earth and the Sun. The Moon blocks out the Sun's rays. No part of the Sun or just a small part of the Sun can be seen.

7

Banneker's Almanac

Before long, Banneker had predicted when the next solar eclipse would take place. He had taught himself astronomy and the math needed to understand the movement of objects in the sky.

Banneker also studied stars, the weather, ocean tides, and medicines. He wrote down the things he discovered. This information was the beginning of his first **almanac**.

What Is an Almanac?

Long ago, the information in almanacs helped sailors guide their boats and farmers plant their crops. Today, almanacs contain information on many different subjects.

An almanac might include:
- dates and times of ocean tides
- solar and lunar eclipses
- weather predictions
- sports information

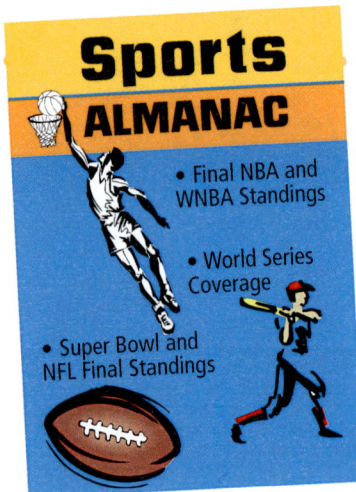

A sports almanac gives information about many different sports.

Banneker decided to try to get his almanac published, or printed in a book. At first no one would publish it, but he did not give up. It was not until Banneker was about 60 years old that his first almanac was published. It had more correct information than most almanacs published at that time. Copies were sold in Pennsylvania, Delaware, Maryland, and Virginia. It was very successful.

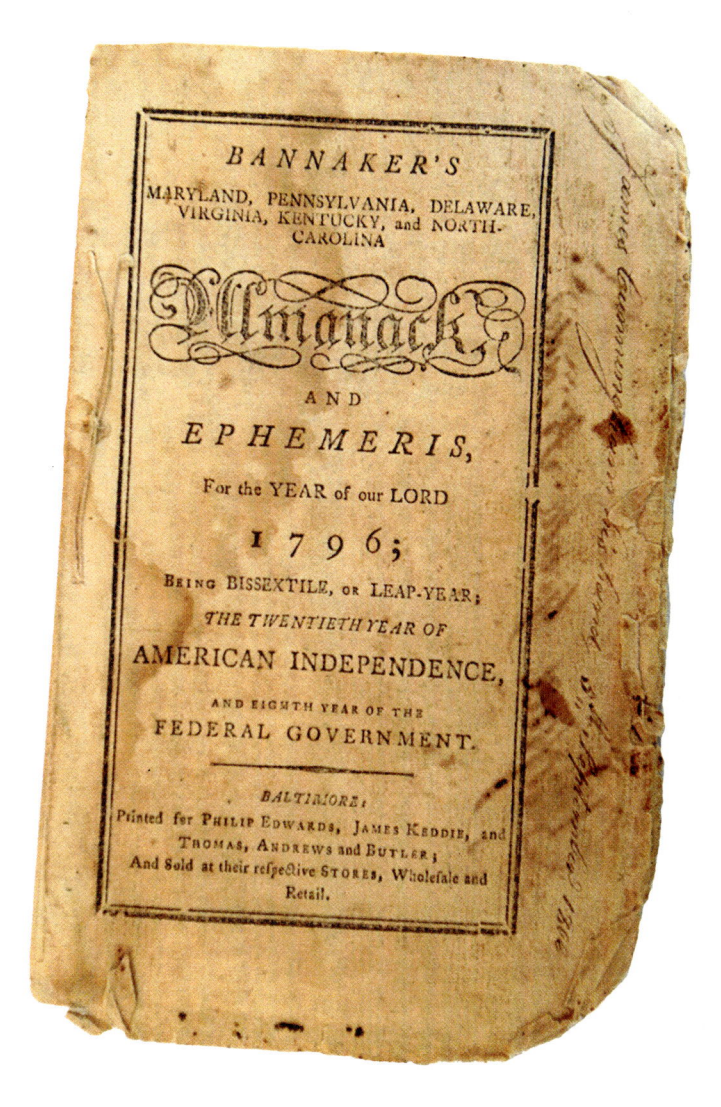

Banneker's almanac from 1796 shows that the spelling of his name varied. Here it is spelled *Bannaker*.

Banneker's Great Adventure

In 1791, when Banneker was about 60 years old, he received a true honor. He was invited to help **survey** the new city of Washington, D.C.

George Washington had become the first president of the United States in 1789. Washington, D.C. was to be the **capital** of the United States. A survey, or a map of the land, had to be made. A surveyor measures and draws lines on the map. Surveyors use telescopes and other tools.

George Washington

The survey team needed someone who understood math and astronomy. This person would help take exact measurements. George Ellicott's cousin, Andrew Ellicott, was in charge of the survey. George Ellicott told his cousin that Benjamin Banneker was right for the job. Banneker was asked to help measure the land where the capital city would be built.

This photograph of Washington, D.C., taken from space, looks similar to the map below.

Banneker worked on the survey team that created this map of Washington, D.C.

Banneker helped with the survey. He learned how to use different survey tools. He checked his measurements again and again to make sure that they were correct. When he was done, he felt that it had been the biggest adventure of his life.

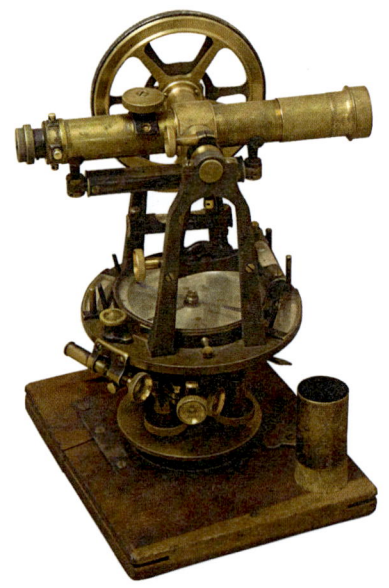

Surveying instruments like this theodolite were used to survey the city of Washington, D.C.

A Timeline of Benjamin Banneker's Life

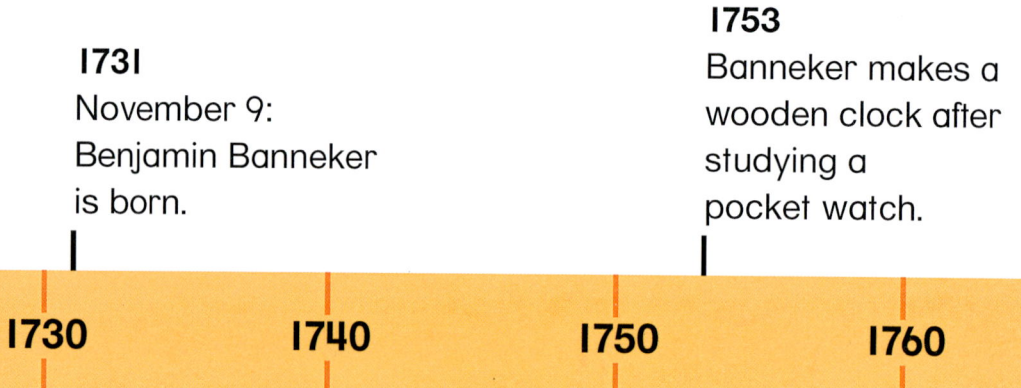

1731
November 9:
Benjamin Banneker
is born.

1753
Banneker makes a
wooden clock after
studying a
pocket watch.

1730　　1740　　1750　　1760

Benjamin Banneker lived until he was almost 75 years old. He was known for having done great things. He taught himself astronomy and math. He helped survey Washington, D.C. Banneker also published six almanacs.

To help people learn more about his life and work in math and science, a museum has been built on the land where Banneker lived. The museum, called the Benjamin Banneker Museum, celebrates the life of this great American thinker.

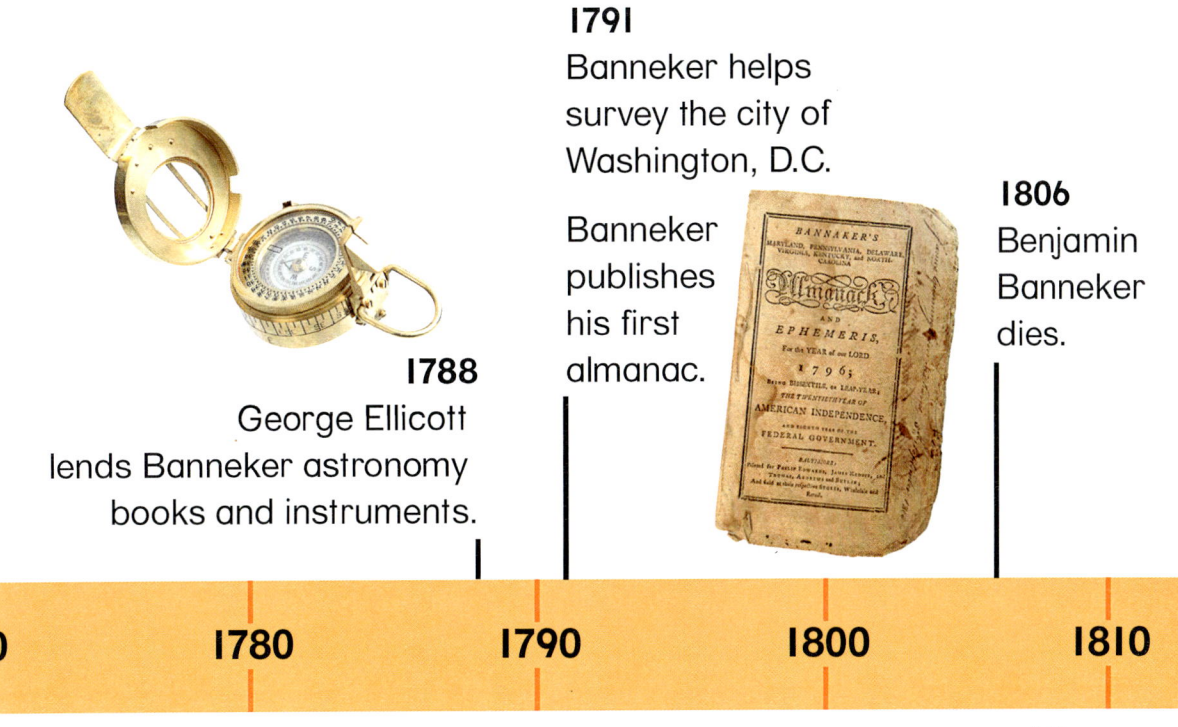

1791
Banneker helps survey the city of Washington, D.C.

Banneker publishes his first almanac.

1788
George Ellicott lends Banneker astronomy books and instruments.

1806
Benjamin Banneker dies.

1780   1790   1800   1810

13

Recommended Reading

Learn more about Benjamin Banneker, astronomy, and almanacs by reading the materials listed below.

Books:

Dear Benjamin Banneker
by Andrea Davis Pinkney and Brian Pinkney (Illustrator)
Voyager Books/Harcourt Brace, September, 1998

What Are You Figuring Now? A Story About Benjamin Banneker
by Jeri Ferris
First Avenue Editions, Lerner Publishing Group, September, 1990

Once Upon a Starry Night: A Book of Constellations
by Jacqueline Mitton and Christina Balit (Illustrator)
National Geographic Children's Books, February, 2004

Web Sites:

The Library of Congress, Local Legacies/Benjamin Banneker Historical Park & Museum:
http://lcweb2.loc.gov/cocoon/legacies/MD/200003116.html

World Almanac for Kids:
www.worldalmanacforkids.com

Official NASA Eclipse site:
eclipse.gsfc.nasa.gov/eclipse.html

Glossary

almanac a book printed each year that gives different types of information, such as weather predictions and solar and lunar eclipses

astronomer a person who studies objects in the sky

capital a city where the highest office of a government is located

eclipses events in which one object in space blocks another object

math the study of measurement and the relationship of quantities using numbers and symbols

predict to tell what will happen in the future

survey to take the measurement of land using special tools to make a map; a map of land that has been carefully measured

Index

almanac   8–9, 13
astronomer   3, 6
astronomy   6, 7, 8, 11, 13
capital   10–11
clock   5, 12
compass   6
Earth   4, 7
eclipse
   lunar   4, 8
   solar   4, 7, 8
Ellicott, Andrew   11
Ellicott, George   6, 11, 13
flute   4
Maryland   3, 9
math   4, 6, 7, 8, 11, 13
Moon   4, 7
planets   7

stars   4, 7, 8
Sun   4, 7
survey   10–13
surveyor   10
survey tools   10, 12
telescope   6, 7
tides   8
violin   4
Washington, D.C.   10–13
Washington, George   10
weather   8